Not Something We Discuss Often

Sarah Cedeño

Harbor Editions
Small Harbor Publishing

Cover art: "Afternoon Tea" by Jen Stein Hauptmann
Cover design by Allison Blevins
Book layout by Hannah Martin and Allison Blevins

Epigraph:
"Carnal Acts" by Nancy Mairs
Copyright © 1990 by Nancy Mairs
Reprinted by permission of Beacon Press, Boston

NOT SOMETHING WE DISCUSS OFTEN
SARAH CEDEÑO
ISBN 978-1-957248-06-6
Harbor Editions,
an imprint of Small Harbor Publishing

for my beautiful boys

CONTENTS

To view your life as blessed does not require you to deny your pain. It simply demands a more complicated vision, one in which a condition or event is not either good or bad but is, rather, both good and bad, not sequentially, but simultaneously.

—Nancy Mairs

Not Something We Discuss Often

THE HEALER

Bob the Healer wore work boots and jeans. In my memory, there's a hardhat on his head.

There were amethysts and rose quartzes and some kind of smoky swirly-white-stones on my cousin's dining room table. I still have them somewhere in a jewelry box, amidst tarnished rings from my youth. There were cups of coffee and packs of cigarettes—Seneca brand —that had been bought on the cheap at the reservation an hour away.

The plan was to heal me. Cory, my boyfriend of about six months, was there; two weeks before, after I'd come out of the shower in a towel and promptly fallen from vertigo, he'd peeled me off the hardwood floors of my grad school apartment. "I'm dying. Just leave me here," I'd said, and then threw up for hours.

A week later, after the MRI, when they told me it wasn't a brain tumor but MS, I told Cory between sips of a martini to leave me before I was in a wheelchair. My aunt brought me a casserole and a book on the power of positive thinking and told me that she knew someone who could help. Another aunt bought me a French press teapot and green tea leaves. Cory stayed.

So here was Bob on a humid, cloudy day that would lead to a thunderstorm we would think was the consequence of healing energy—the kind that would remove the lesions from the part of my brain that controlled my balance. Though in reality, the most that would happen to fix my brain already had: an

11

intravenous infusion of steroids that turned the fizz of the lesion to plaque, a scar that would make me wobbly as a toddler at inopportune moments. But at that time, every bolt of lightning was a prayer. My mom tapped her cigarette in the ashtray and told me to stop giggling. Bob reminded me to uncross my legs so not to impede the energy. The smoke from my mother's, my aunt's, and my cousin's Senecas ambled into the air. Somewhere amidst the three of them was a rosary.

As I type this, I begin to list the things left unmitigated by Bob the Healer: My fingertips have gone numb, as has half my arm, making the typing of this both clumsy and frustrating. The vision in my right eye has smeared over, filmy, like Vaseline, so I have taken advantage of wearing a pirate's eye-patch to entertain my children. I've been squeezed in the "MS Hug"—around my ribcage as though I were prey, precious and necessary for survival—and thought I was having an anxiety or heart attack. My weakened immune system sprouted shingles around my midsection, keeping me from wearing a bra, making me feel like a burn victim. I have no scars, though. My hands quake coffee cups, leaving drips around my house. The big toe on my right foot is so numb that I removed the entire nail with clippers to resolve an ingrown toenail. In fact, over the past ten years, the worst I've felt was numb. Numb.

I sat in a chair (Legs uncrossed! Arms loosely by my side!). My mother and aunt were concerned and scolding in the gentle way Italians scold.

"Mingya, Sarah, do what he says."

"Shh. Quit your joking. And I mean it."

"Do you want this to work, or no?"

It was, after all, very serious. Cory was the ultimate spectator. His wholesome face and placid expression gave off an air of safety to my family. His hair, curly and thick, was charming in a hearty, protective way. And as a good boyfriend, he was expected to agree with whatever my mother and aunt said. My cousin would nod, too—her house was littered with what you might find in the home of someone who practiced Reiki. Aura charts. Crystals. Massage tables. Spirits.

I couldn't help but giggle. Bob was wearing a flannel and smelled of sweat and dirty clothes. I liked him. *He was funny*, I remember writing in a journal that I cannot, now, remember where I've put. He was matter of fact discussing the healing, as if he were talking about patching drywall or measuring wainscoting—*measure twice, cut once!*

"Take these," he said, plunking an amethyst and rose-colored stone into my palm. "You ought to wash them every couple days. Soap and water." I nodded. Apparently, we all leak energy like rusty spigots.

I liked holding the stones in my hands. I was sentimental, and talismans were more about memories than spirituality. "They're for protection," he added, to which I nodded again, more vigorously.

He started at the crown of my head and swept his hand, about two inches away from my body, along my side. Something had happened to him to give him healing powers, and he told us about it—maybe it was a lightning strike? I imagine it now: Bob on a farm, changing tractor oil. Or shingling a roof. I picture him as the rest of us, handling business as usual until the moment that demanded transformation. What was his moment? A broken marriage, maybe? An ill daughter? The loss of a friend? And then, suddenly, he was ordained by a bolt from above.

Thunder rumbled.

"Do you feel anything? How do you feel?" my mother asked. I didn't feel anything, except for some warmth radiating from Bob's hand.

"It's warm," I said, trying. I tried to do lots of things at that time, convince others I would be okay. I tried to keep my eyes closed, so I could keep my face straight. I did, though, open them to see the thinning hair at the crest of Bob's head, his freckles and crepe-y skin near his eyelids. Sheer curtains billowed like in the music video of a slow song. Rain dropped like timpani. One should expect to hear cicadas. That day, it seemed impossible that I would be healed, but equally impossible that I would not.

Lightning made my mother jump. "Whoa," she said. My cousin dragged from her cigarette and nodded again like *This is proof you will be healed*. I think I remember, at one point, lying on the dining room table as though at my wake, with Bob's hand hovering over my third eye, but who knows. I wouldn't be able to write about this moment for over ten years, and the memory of it now feels obscured by the fact that I appear as able today as I did then, though at the time, the moment of diagnosis came to my family as a death sentence.

Bob washed his hands after he healed me. My aura was yellow, he said.

I would discover over time that others needed me to heal more than I did. My mother's family normally emoted as though we were living our last day, with constant *Watch the cars!* as you looked both ways from the curb or *I love you with all my heart!* when hanging up the phone, so to them, by having an unpredictable disease, I was balancing on the centerline of a highway I'd never meant to walk down. I remember family saying *Cory is a saint* so many times after my diagnosis. Everyone became aglow and obsessed with holiness. After my diagnosis, it was not a strange occurrence at family picnics for my Aunt Orry to stroke my hair and call me her angel before I downed a third glass of boxed wine and karaoked Eminem. My mother's family doesn't leak energy, they throw it on you in buckets. Their love is fierce.

I was too young to think about canes or wheelchairs. I drank green tea, took high-test vitamin D, injected chemicals into any fatty surface of my body, and avoided hot showers, resenting it all. I did keep the stones in my pockets for months after, moving them from jeans to jeans each morning. The only time they were washed was when I forgot to remove them from my pockets before my pants hit the laundry machine.

On that day, we all hoped. It was dramatic and anticlimactic. We talked about the dinners we'd have that night. Sauce. Burgers on the grill. Bob sat at the table, his large hands wrapped around a mug of coffee. Cory looked at me, dying to debrief over beer or vodka-cranberry, finally able to laugh out loud.

At some point, no matter how many lesions I accumulated, no matter how many exacerbations came and went, I lowered my expectations of what the disease would do to me. Sometimes, though, when I'm trying to get Cory to take a walk with me, I say, "Who knows how many more walks I have left?" It's been so long since the thunderstorm and the belief that energy and rosaries could take disease away. None of us mentioned the fact that I continued to have MS after the healing—not even my mother and my aunt, who finished a pack of cigarettes at the table that day.

The pastel stones nearly wore holes in my jean pockets, but now I would say I didn't expect them to do much else. It's been so long since I carried them that if I were to rub them between my hands on the couch at night, Cory would ask where they'd come from.

ON SMALL

I

I am large and in charge. When I inhale, I take in all the air in the room, and when I let it out, wind whips through the hair of others—through the wisps of black on my neurologist's head or the mop of caramel blond on my oldest son. People wonder how I've come to be such a force.

II

But that's not true at all. I have small lungs with little power. When I blow into the flow meter, doctors think I'm not trying. If I make it to 40, I will not extinguish the candles in one breath. I can wear my son's shoes in a pinch. I can buy training bras and t-shirts from the girls' section of Target. Students call me adorable and look at me like I'm a puppy when I have to stand on my toes to reach a bagel in the lunch line. This type of gaze feels comfortable only because it's normal.

III

You might think I'm in the four-foot range. I'm not. But in the playback of an interview with one of my favorite writers, I sound even smaller than four feet, and the further into the hour-long interview, the smaller my voice shrinks next to her rasp. Whatever questions about writing I ask diminish between her breaths. I can hardly listen.

IV

Small, a word that makes me think of Pooter, the youngest of the children who lived a couple houses down from me as a child. *Pooter*. Think of the name.

Pooter—pale and blond—wore nothing but a diaper (the same one all day) and no shoes though the sidewalks in our neighborhood were littered with shards of beer bottles. He ran and ran to keep up with his siblings who always left him behind.

V

Being small is like being a penny. Something to steal from the world when happened upon. Throw into a fountain for luck. I have fit into the pockets of many men, have felt myself shrink like a raisin and put someplace I cannot crawl out of.

VI

Like the last drop in my grandmother's old wine glasses, the meager drop I can never get because by the time it's reached my lips, it's disappeared along the curve. The drop that in two minutes' time will re-accumulate and tempt me, but no matter because anything in that small a quantity can't satisfy.

VII

My son, this morning: "Mom, why is your scarf so big?" My mother, on Christmas: "Sarah, you look like a hobo in that thing." A student: "Professor, don't you think that scarf is a little, um, large for you?" My colleague: "Is that like a security blanket?" But I love the onset of cold so I can wrap up in lengths of fabric after a summer exposed in heat—my bony knees, my twiggy shoulders. Instead: a scarf, usually plaid, usually wool, doubled over on itself, smelling like the coffee I've spilled, piled up and up and up against my chin. I hide there.

VIII

Not unlike so many women my size—my mother, my neurologist, the department chair, Hillary Clinton—women of power who say *stand tall* or *eat something* or *take care* because they know the small cannot afford poor posture.

IX

And shrinking. My son has heard both my mother and me say humans stop growing at age 18 and begin shrinking at age 30. Funny, the things I pass along when I'm not sure of the validity. He shows me the size I will be before I die using the two inches of space between his forefinger and thumb.

X

Small enough I cannot create a disaster to affect many other than myself. My messes are contained, cocooned, fit in a whisper at night before I go to sleep. I steal things, but only things that aren't for sale: diner mugs, hearts, newspapers left behind on a table. Things no one will notice. Things small enough to carry.

XI

The doctor calls me little as he sketches a bar graph of my stress hormones: serotonin, norepinephrine, dopamine—the same graph he's drawn at each of my appointments. They increase in size like skyscrapers on the back of his prescription tablet. "When we have a patient who's already little," he says, "and who has now lost seven pounds, we're concerned given her history of depression." I look around to see if someone else is in the room. But I'm her. Times like these, I eat only enough to keep my stomach from growling. He lassos the skyscrapers with his felt tip pen and prescribes me pills.

XII

My grandmother looks down at me from a black and white photo tucked in the corner of my mahogany mirror. She looks like Tinkerbell. Her pale skin and light eyes show no evidence of electroshock, Lithium, mind-altering meds. The other night, a large man who's lived on my block since I was a child and I've always been fearful of stopped me on the corner of Main Street to tell me I looked like a star who flew down in a harness during a London production of Peter Pan. I imagine the actress suspended above the audience—stick-legs dangling—magic and out of reach like the tiniest firefly.

AFTERMATH

597 South Oakland Ave, Sharon, PA, is full of antique dressers and tables and clocks, family photos, artwork that Grandma and Aunt Andrea (we call her Andy) painted. They painted owls, a replica of Picasso's *Seated Nude*, portraits of family, paintings of dead deer, paintings of landscapes I've never seen in real life. And there are my great grandfather's medical books, diaries, newspapers, beaded rosaries and wooden rosaries and jeweled rosaries and plastic rosaries. And cardboard boxes, my aunt's clothes heaped on kitchen counters and the bathroom floor and in the shower, more cardboard boxes, taxes from 1948 through 1976 and from two or three years ago bound in paper or in vinyl, baggies full of pennies clumped together by age and something sticky.

Something sticky everywhere—in my nose, on my latex gloves, crowding any thought I might have like, what did I just step on? Or, hey—is that Polish pottery? Or, how is life worth living? Cobwebs so thick they look like strips of finger-knitting canopied over the whole mess. Czechoslovakian cookbooks and sour cream containers. A yogurt from a few years ago with its sour spoon. Sour everything. Old Isotoner slippers, crystal candlesticks, Japanese pottery from Great Uncle Jack, plants so neglected they look like twisted paper lunch bags growing out of white dirt, tins of mail order cookies expired in 1996 and never opened, five slow cookers, still in their boxes—gifts that were never given.

Mouse poop. Everywhere.

Andy had no children. Her husbands had died. This is why she willed the house and all of its contents to my father, who jokes that he is being punished.

"I've researched hoarding," my father says when he first opens the front door. "Aunt Andy was not a hoarder." We cannot step in.

My father explains, now, *it's laziness,* she became overwhelmed with the mess, which in her diaries she refers to as "the condition of the house." We can only stand on the perimeter and stare into it. It isn't something we can touch. My father says it is not a mental illness. But he looks from the perimeter. Even though we are knee-deep, he keeps himself on the perimeter.

A group of workers—only men—shovel their way through each room. They call my name to alert me to photographs or diaries. The name of their company is Aftermath. I admire the person who came up with the name. "This is a seven out of ten on the scale," they say. They usually clean crime scenes. They flip through pages of books for money, inform me when something looks valuable, and I imagine some valuable things still ended up in those shovels. I can't save it all though, can I? Can I sift through the mess in handfuls like a squirrel, stash my own mess to the side?

My father walks around with a perpetually stunned look on his face. He scratches his beard and makes jokes. "I'm hungry," he says as he struggles over an open and full container of leftovers on top of a mountain of plastic bags on top of a box of club crackers on top of mildewed towels. Our white HAZMAT suits are pristine in the stale air. I imagine the glorious paradise of an open window and a drink of purified iced water. There is a note on the refrigerator from Andy. She wrote: *Do not open the refrigerator. It is full of food and has not worked in five years.* We aren't sure when it was written, but the paper has yellowed. We couldn't get the door to the refrigerator open. There are clothes and dirty dishes and books surrounding it.

During this, the first trip, workers fill a forty and a thirty-yard dumpster with the first floor of Andy's belongings. This is her layer, what accumulated after Great Grandma died in 1994.

When we get home, I text my father a picture of my study closet: newspapers and books and frames and photographs and baby blankets and posters and the gift bags from every gift I've received in the past two years. I clean it out that day and tell him I can't judge Andy. Had I been alone, with no children, with no family at all to speak of . . . I mean, *I can see how it would happen to a ninety-year-old woman.* I cringe as I text it. I can't fathom it, and yet I can.

I speak of Andy suddenly to my husband over dinner or when I'm about to fall asleep as though we are mid-conversation about her.

"Did you know she couldn't reach the light fixtures to replace blown bulbs and she sat in the dark all winter?" I don't need to clarify who "she" is anymore. She finds her way into my mind and my mouth at unexpected moments. She litters my life.

After I clean out my closet, I text my father a new picture. He texts back, *I thought you were going to clean it out?*

Eh. Turns out, I needed most of it, I text, staring at the plaid gift bag with the tear in the corner. It is filled with balled up tissue paper.

I tell my students story is born of the perfect storm of character and circumstance. That readers like inevitable tragedy. It's why we watch the news. It's why I'll walk all the way down Park Avenue with my son and my father to watch firefighters extinguish the attic of an old white house, the smell of a burning house both delicious and frightening, the smoky cotton haze like an exhale from the home. South Oakland Avenue is the site of Andy's perfect storm—a tragedy of illness and isolation. And we are living in the aftermath.

On our next trip to Andy's house, my father tells my aunts and uncles that Andy is my kindred spirit. Everyone laughs nervously as I pick up random items to bring home—a small Red Rose Tea squirrel collectors call a whimsy, a silver figurine of a gnome playing the fiddle with a cat pawing its knee, a few cookbooks, a doorbell and doorknocker, the tile from the front door.

I don't have Andy's illness, but I can understand her need to hold what came before she was alone. At some point, she couldn't tell what came before her mother died and what came after.

In class couple of weeks ago, we shared our favorite poems. I read my students a William Stafford poem called "The Widow," "Maybe nothing should move. Maybe this day, the stillness begins." The photos and artwork on her wall are in the same order as they were in photographs I find from the seventies and eighties and nineties and are of people who left her behind or painted by people who left her behind.

I tell my students Andy's story. They ask me for updates when I return from weekend trips to Sharon, PA. I'm not good at family secrets.

Sometimes, in her diary entries and letters, there are marks of hindsight in different colored ink, as though she has read and reread and revised her story. Sometimes she says she misses her family horribly. Sometimes she says her family makes her miserable. I imagine her watching the detritus grow around her exponentially and feel her suffocation. I look around my study: three bowls of binder clips, five clipboards full of drafts I won't revisit, seven staplers in various sizes, bricks I stole from places of meaning, 10 vintage coasters stacked on my desk, writing magazines from 2000 and 2005 and in between and beyond, and five boxes full of stationery I'll never send—or maybe I will, someday.

One time, in her diary amidst others now stacked in my study, my Aunt Andy prays for cancer.

I can't be angry with my father for ignoring this element of mental illness. He is protecting himself—from culpability, from sorrow, from regret, from his own doubts. He knows about mental illness. My grandmother had bipolar disorder. But this is not something we discuss often. And his brother, the doctor, is the only one who will recall my grandmother's episodes, how he and my father were sent to Andy's for summers when my grandmother was at her worst. I find a letter tucked in the pages of the Slovak-American cookbook from when Andy stayed with my grandmother during a tough time. At that point, my grandmother had four children. I can see the deterioration between Andy and my grandmother, the lack of understanding between the two, how Andy compared my grandmother to a toddler, called attention to her temper, to how she slept and swore and ate only toast and yogurt.

I started taking antidepressants when I was twelve, and sometimes my mother would say to me, "Everyone gets sad, Sarah." I could barely eat and didn't want to do anything but hide in my room. A day later she would hold me and ask me, "What is wrong with you?" My father would roll his eyes as I cried, but later, she would tell me that he was scared. We set all our boundaries through fear.

I instruct my students to write fiction about what they most fear. Last summer, I thought my worst fear was the pedophile whose yard backs up to mine. Now, I fear that threats are even closer to home.

Andy wasn't born a hoarder. There are photo albums from the twenties and thirties when she was in elementary school. In one photograph, she is an angel in a play, and then there are photo albums from the seventies of Andy standing in a pristine kitchen next to her husband in front of her ivory refrigerator with a steel whisk in her hand. She is wearing an apron and a smile. There is someone by her side. Their counter is bare, and I imagine she has recently swept it free of crumbs.

On the second trip to Sharon, we ascend to the second floor, which proves worse. It was her private living space, and she still, deep down, had a sense of domestic decency—what was appropriate for first floor versus second-floor living. It's the way we vacuum and mop the downstairs floors but leave the upstairs floors alone. Once the shovels disturb the clothing, the smell goes from stale and suspicious to putrid and sharp. Soiled underwear, bras on doorknobs, cardboard boxes, takeout container after takeout container. And her poodle had to go to the bathroom somewhere. Her other poodle took up his final resting place under a four-foot pile of clothes. I imagine one day Andy couldn't find him, and her diary said she was having trouble breathing. Now, we can only see the bones.

My aunt tells me I need to write a novel called *Andrea's Dilemma.*

In a book I almost throw away, I find a paper dated 2010, marked OBIT, on which Andy drafted her own obituary. In Andy's list of the predeceased is everyone she held dear. The list of who survives her is too short and summed up in one line: 8 nieces and nephews, 19 grandnieces and grandnephews. She refers to herself as an "unheralded philanthropist." She kept all of us at bay with cards and checks. When she died, she had nearly a million dollars.

"She didn't have to live like this," we all say. We didn't know why we couldn't visit, until we couldn't visit her anymore.

In one diary entry, Andy tells how her dog groomer broke into her house because she thought Andy was dead. Andy was so angry and mortified that someone entered her house—and so frightened they would come in again—that she didn't sleep for a week.

On the third trip to Sharon, and with the first floor swept clean and the Persian rugs rolled up and hauled into a dumpster, the house begins to look almost habitable, and this is when the real despair hits. With the windows opened for the first time in decades and the debris pulled down, the sun hits the concentric rectangle pattern of the hardwood floors and there's a hint of reflection. This is how Andy would have remembered it from her youth. The fireplace, the built-in bookshelves and nooks in the library all made to heat and organize and hold lives comfortably, even Andy's.

An Aftermath worker holds a dead rat from the basement a few feet in front of my face, its tail stiff like the handle of a pinwheel and its body a deflated version of the hairy rodents I've only ever seen on *Dirty Jobs*.

My father describes everything here as "petrified."

"Rat's not that old, but at least he's not squealing," the worker says. I've already run to the other side of the room, covering my mouth, and out come three more, on a shovel.

I've found families of mice, here, but not living mice, their bones clean and smooth. I've stepped on one, felt it crush beneath my foot.

"None survived," the project foreman says, tipping the rats from the shovel into an industrial-sized garbage can.

Three weeks later, when the U-Haul pulls up in front of my house, it's black and rainy outside. It's December, and inside I've decorated for Christmas. Crayola-colored lights on the tree. The stockings Andy crocheted for all of us when we were young hang from my stair balusters.

The contents of 597 have moved to a U-Haul. My father calls the back room of my second floor the "staging area," a room we don't use. I'd spent all day cleaning for Andy's stuff as if for a houseguest— washing the windows and mopping the floors, emptying the room of clutter. When my father rolls up the door of the U-Haul, my mother and sister cover their noses. A whole houseful of Andy's furniture, mirrors, memorabilia, mail-order steam grills, about to parade into my already-full house.

It is 5:30 and soon, we have a Christmas party at my friend Anne's house. I am supposed arrive early to help set up.

My sons watch as the contents of the U-Haul filter into the house. I pace back and forth as my brother-in-law and nephew ask me, "Where? Where does this go?" and my mother shakes her head, says, "Oh my god."

My father says, "You wanted this, Sarah. You told me not to get rid of it."

I hadn't been the only one, sifting through this stuff— my mother and sister had, too, recognizing treasure in the wreck: carved wooden puzzles, my great grandmother's Singer bust, Czechoslovakian pottery and scrapbooks. And furniture. And lamps and paintings and bags full of pictures that were so soiled I asked the cleaners to put them in a new bag to hide them from me so I would forget how filthy they were and not put them in the dumpster. Amidst these papers, I'll find a three-page spread about Andy in the

Woodstock Union High School Newsletter at her retirement from teaching in 1987 at the age of 65. Her students admired her. I imagine she was strict and sweet, both generous and guarded, congenial and no-nonsense. A guidance counselor named Suzy says of her, recalling a student who was on drugs and wreaking havoc on his family, "Andy took the boy in and kept him at her house for a year. She helped him get through school." A few paragraphs later, Andy's quoted: "My father was a 24-hour doctor. He had a tough, tough life. He was home so seldom. I decided I wanted to be a home maker, to eventually marry and have 13 kids."

Her holiday messages on our answering machine were the texture of fine sandpaper. We never knew what she sat amidst.

Immediately, I try sending small hallway tables home with my sister, a cardboard box full of silver with anyone who would have it, and thankfully succeed at sending my great grandfather's WWI and my great uncle's WWII helmets and boxes of their dress whites with my father, though he will march them back into my house not even a week later.

"Mom, you wanted that craft table," I try.

And to my father-in-law: "Can you please take this end table? What is that sludge on it?"

My sons are giddy, jumping in the U-Haul as it empties out; their voices echo into the night, asking which bedroom set is theirs. Later, we'll assemble the early 1900s mahogany twin beds with curved footboards to situate in their room that's decked out in *Star Wars*, *Angry Birds*, Sabres and Buffalo Bills gear. When the U-

Haul is nearly empty, I realize it's so large we all could do cartwheels from front to back. And it had been full.

As the "moving crew" carries armfuls through my front door, the looks on their faces turn to panic. The staging area has filled up. When I walk up the stairs, I imagine the floor of Andy's room, as we now call it, collapsing beneath 6 dressers, 20 file cabinet drawers, 4 lamps, 4 steamer trunks and boxes and boxes of scrapbooks and pictures and keepsakes.

I try harder to pawn items off on my family—gold-laced china black with excrement, broken clocks, tennis rackets, my great grandfather's framed satin med-school diplomas.

My son's the first taker. "I'll take this!" Johnny says from the front porch, hoisting an old wooden valet stand under his arm. He carries it over the threshold and up the stairs to his bedroom. Little bugs and cobwebs cling to the feet like felt floor protectors. By the next night, where my great grandfather had hung his starched doctor's shirts will have become the perfect place to display my son's hockey jersey. We will also find two large boxes of my great grandfather's medical tools —forceps, circumcision instruments, tonsil tools, surgical scissors.

The larger pieces—two secretary desks, two kitchen tables, and a 20" x 30" box of WWI photos—wedge in the shrinking space of my front parlor.

"Hoarding is hereditary," my dad says, and though he's joking as he walks out the door with my mother, it takes all I have to keep myself from throwing myself on his back and begging him not to go.

Though part of me feels happy and full with all the family history in my home, another part of me begins to itch. My house is full of orphan cobwebs and foreign dust. I consider wearing one of the leftover paper respirators from the clean-out that have somehow also landed in my front parlor. Streaks of black run down my arm and my nails are perfect black French tips. I turn the light off in the front room. It is 6:30 and the tree lights shine on the many filthy surfaces of desks and end tables and a kitchen table. *Merry Christmas, Aunt Andy*, I think.

My husband's eyes widen as he shuts the front door behind everyone—my sons are gone, too, for a sleepover with their grandparents—away from the condition of the house. We have a party to go to. A drip of sweat falls from the tip of my husband's nose and I bury my face into his neck, away from the smell.

Anne's house is clean and bright, full of cheer and wine and Lebanese appetizers. I smell like Dove body wash and shea butter hair products and no one would guess where I've just come from. Through the joyful faces and clinking bottles, I see the dark windows of my house, where I've left my dog Molly with the mess, and if I look hard enough, by the glow of the streetlights, I might be able to see the outlines of all the extra furniture. I cannot hold back. I tell many acquaintances what transpired just before the party—though it's not a story about me I'm telling; I tell a tragedy about Andy.

My husband drinks quite a bit at the party, and it's likely because he knows what awaits him at home. The rain has turned to snow by the time we leave, and though it's cold, I hesitate to go inside. Our house is a big old

Victorian, but I know that the high ceilings are no match for the smell that's to come.

As I make my way through the staging area that I now call "Andy's room" to get to my bedroom, I imagine bugs and mice ascending my legs. My cat will nest in this room for months, and I'll be afraid to pet her and even more paranoid she will jump on our bed at night with bugs hiding in her fur.

My husband tries to keep the door to Andy's room closed tonight, but the cat scratches at the wood until we have to open it. I tell him it's cruel to leave her in there. And from then on, we sleep with the door to Andy's room open.

A PICTURE OF NATURAL DEMISE

Aside from the front porch, the hundred-year-old silver maple was my favorite part of the house. When everyone called me melodramatic about the thought of the old tree coming down, I would sift back through my Facebook albums examining the many photos I'd taken of it. In the summer, Molly, our German shepherd, would lie regally beneath it, and in the fall, the dead leaves looked like confetti and gave me hope. In winter, even when its blackened arms against sky made me think of failing synapses and nervous system and illness —what my MRIs continued to reveal—there was something in the fact that it was still standing that said *strength*.

Everyone on our block knew our tree. The tree, actually two trees that had grown together, now threatened to come apart. The center, where they'd joined all the way to the stump, was rotting out. *Squirrels live there*, I thought, a way of reasoning for both the tree's staying and for its coming down. "If you knock on it, it's hollow," my husband argued. "It'll crush the Subaru," he said. Our horticulturist neighbor had warned us three years earlier, when we'd bought the house, that the tree had been rotting for a long time and threatened to take out at least three garages and six neighborhood children when it fell.

The tree was like an octopus with limbs stretching wildly toward the sky. The two largest branches formed the shape of a wine glass perched on the trunk, its hearty stem. It cast enough shade for two back yards. It was majestic. Thinking on it now, I could have staged a protest with the two women who lived on either side of me. We could have chained ourselves to the trunk. And yet maybe the harder I fought, the worse it would feel when we had to unchain ourselves and watch the tree come down anyway.

I recognize, only now, that in my quest for control and power, a new philosophy had overtaken me to try everything I'd never done before—basically, anything my mother might have scared me away from my entire life: climbing trees, walking alone at night, driving places by myself, talking on the phone or showering during a thunderstorm, or chatting openly with strangers. The way life was going—with multiple sclerosis slowly numbing my hands and stealing bits of my vision—I was staring off the edge of disease at what? A Cane? Blindness? Needing Cory or my sons to wheel me around? Or even perhaps the anticlimactic, nothing out of the ordinary?

The evening before, I photographed my boys and the neighborhood kids posed against the tree and hanging on the tire swing. Even the teenaged boy humored me. After nightfall, my friend Anne and I sat beneath its branches in patio chairs with wine. After some begging, Cory perched the ladder against one of the tree's huge arms, and Anne and I climbed up for a photo I desperately wanted and sincerely believed would be beautiful.

My legs squeezed the limb so tight for fear of falling that it left bruises on my thighs for weeks. Anne and I attempted to gaze seriously into the distance for the photo, as though this were a normal and natural thing we were doing—thinking about the sad sacrifice of trees—but in the photo, the flash caught our eyes, and we bore the shocked expressions of raccoons.

We'd been up there for a minute at most. I'd caught sight of the lightning crack behind the tall steeple of the Presbyterian Church not a block away. An early summer storm was coming. I imagined my mother hiding in her stairwell, the only place in her house without a window. I thought how perfect it would be if the tree came down in the storm, stricken with a bolt and smoldering in our yard, to surrender before defeat, a picture of natural demise.

It took two days to bring it down. After, our yard was stark, like nuclear fallout. Molly wandered gingerly around as though she'd been dropped on Jupiter. The sun was heavy, and her shade tree had become hamster bedding. That summer was so dry, every tomato on my plant split before it was ready to pick. I could feel that the oxygen the tree supplied was gone. The neighbors shook their heads and said, "What a shame." You would expect to hear an echo out there, in my back yard, a graveyard of tree chunks.

The relentless sun bleached our front yard, and the weather reports read: DROUGHT, so Cory spent inordinate amounts of time dragging the hose around the front yard, trying to green up the lawn and save the diseased magnolia he'd reluctantly planted for me one Mother's Day. That summer, our water bill blossomed.

One night, after having asked Cory to clean up the tree carcass many times, I was in the back yard amidst maple logs the diameter of prize-winning watermelons. I wanted the mess moved. My mother would have told me *Wait for Cory to do that*. But Cory always said *Soon*.

Had Cory said *Never*, it would have been better than saying *Soon*. I would not wait. I would do it myself.

The numbness on my hands had crawled up my arms and left them feeling covered in paraffin wax. It had become clear I had no choice but to look ahead into a time that would startle me—a summer during which I would blame my endless crying on my MS drugs, and my youngest son would say to my oldest: "It's okay, Johnny, she's just sad because of her medicine." Every song from that summer still makes my nose burn. I knew I was trying to maintain appearances, sometimes not asking for help so I could be angry when no help was offered. I knew I often skipped doses so I could drink wine without struggling with both a hangover and the side effects from the meds. There were times that summer I'd wait until everyone was sleeping, assemble the needle, and inject myself alone in the dining room: a pitiful, self-indulgent ritual during which I cried and wanted to believe I was the only one who suffered from my illness.

The night was clear, of course, because clouds might have meant rain would quench the thirst. And quenching wasn't in the cards that summer. The crickets weren't loud yet, but the tree frogs were. I stared longingly at the shadows of the glorious trees in my neighbors' back yards. And beyond those, at the quaint glowing windows of the Victorian houses that allow you to believe the feeling in every home was happy.

The logs weren't just heavy, they were *fucking heavy*. My goal was to at least move them to the outskirts of the yard so that Molly could move about and, should the neighborhood children dare to ever traverse the landscape again, they wouldn't impale themselves on silver maple rigor mortis.

The first hunks were easy, and I was able to toss them. (I started small.) The supremely heavy chunks (those I was told to keep as seats at the bonfire), I rolled to the edge and hefted up on their bottoms. The mediocre pieces were the hardest—big enough for me to struggle, small enough for me to insist on heaving into a pile. I hadn't thought to change out of my flip-flops.

A couple lighter logs fell from my hands onto my feet since I couldn't really tell if I was gripping adequately— the pain made me pick a heavier log and throw it so hard against the others I'd grunt. I couldn't worry about the army of carpenter ants I displaced. I'd entered destruction mode, imagining my face in the dirt without having fallen. I lifted and threw until I was sobbing with wood bits and dirt all over my face. I remembered when I was young: my mother wanting her space changed, pushing couches up stairs before my father came home from work, her olive face red. I remembered the secrets I held onto for her, those that gave her power. My dad would say, "Why didn't you wait until I came home to rearrange the house?" In some ways, if she wanted it done, she'd had no choice. She wasn't looking for permission. I remember wanting to do further damage than what had been done when the tree came down. And I wanted to do it myself. But I'd already reached the outer limits of my destruction: cut knees, enormous slivers, a black toe, bruises and scratches that lasted for days. My mother asked where they come from.

There was a moment I wondered if I'd heard Cory coming to help. Maybe I wanted him to find me in a heap so I could say, "See? Here is a mess." Maybe I worried what kind of mess I'd become, what would he do then, and what would I be able to do for myself? The water still hissed through the hose, and Cory was still in front, trying to maintain curb appeal.

Molly carried a large stick over in her mouth and dropped it next to me. I sat down on one of the bonfire tree stumps, sweaty and panting. Molly licked my feet, and I tried to get her to look me in the eye so she would know that I saw her, but she, hopelessly submissive, just leaned her butt against me asking for a scratch. That night we gazed at the impossible space where the tree had been, and it was like staring into the sun.

ON THE ROAD'S SHOULDER

I'm sorry for the table scraps I give the dog when you're not looking, how I scrape the meat sludge from your sauce plate into the dog bowl, how she laps it up because she knows it is deserved, the last of her ten years on this earth. I'm sorry for dimming the ceiling light you've just blazed on, for preferring the lamps my mother gave me that I nestle in the corners. I'm sorry for having turned my back to you so many nights, for having blamed the oppressive heat and tied the curtains back when you'd rather them closed. I'm sorry for having enjoyed all the breeze that came in through the windows while you snored into the hallway. I'm sorry, too, and I'll say again and again that I'm sorry for the glass of wine that turns into four and into five until I've sunken into someone who is not me. That I will make the "just jelly" sandwich for Sammy instead of slathering peanut butter on one side. I'm sorry not all the meals I make contain a protein. And I'm sorry for the heels of my feet, scratchy against your calves at night. I'm sorry for so often saying yes to others that I have to say no to you. I'm sorry for apologizing for things I continue to do, for dragging what you mean out of you like the entrails of a buck on the road's shoulder.

RE·TURN

/rə'tərn/ v. 1. Having dreamt of her husband again,after so long almost chronically lying beside him: his neck and its delicate silver cross resting in the soft pocket between clavicles. The taste of blood: as when feeling chain links around her tongue, between her teeth, watching the healthy pulse beneath his ear. 2. Stepping over a puddle toward him, and, after the ice has melted, finding her worn leather boots are enough —and safe, just the little bit of muck that seeps in at the toe making her heels desirous with fire. Or even accepting the warmth of a favorite sweater on which her clumsy fingers have sewn a patch. 3. Relief: as when she's sitting in her garage, numb like cotton with the engine on, tempted to close the door, but fixating instead on his efficient piles of screwdrivers and years of accumulated wood. Her sons' skateboards, too, wasting under the workbench, scolding her. 4. Remembering: almost stepping into a forest of timid branches/diseased bramble, but instead, collapsing into their bed, her only destination, staring off at an older version of herself. And her husband, carrying her lovingly. Tenderly, like a small burden.

FUTURE CARE INSTRUCTIONS FOR YOUR WIFE WITH MULTIPLE SCLEROSIS

When I can no longer grasp the tweezers to pull at the fine blond blades between my eyebrows, please look closely. Pluck them all—imagine them as the weeds in the garden we never got to, the sumac growing up through the rhododendron. The mole on my left cheek —if you see me run my fingers over it as though I can still feel a hair breaking through, ask me about it before my finger rubs it raw. The tiny stubborn hairs beneath our chins that my mother and I fuss about, pull harder on those.

Humor me when I want to show our boys what my handwriting used to be, a specific if unwieldy cursive/print hybrid.

Two ice cubes in my coffee, please. Black. Please sit with me with a mug of water or milk in your hands if you don't want any. Pretend it is coffee. Our son Johnny likes his with two scoops of hot chocolate and some sugar if you make it for him.

Please leave some lamps glowing from their corners so I can see on my way to bed. They are beacons, and the dogs who love me have become obstacles.

Please don't stop trimming my nails if I joke that you've gotten my finger. I still like to laugh.

For our son Sam, sometimes sneak him a snack at night. Make your way from the kitchen, up the stairs, through the laundry room by night light, tap softly on the door or call *Sam-Sam*, so as not to scare him.

Please make sure I'm not wearing flip flops if I insist on some summer night that I can walk home. If I trip over the train tracks, ice my lip before I look in a mirror. Clean the blood before I taste copper.

Please scrub my scalp with shampoo and let the suds rinse through, but don't shampoo the ends. No sulfates, please.

Brush my tongue as well as my teeth.

In the summer, run the razor up my shins and over my knees, and be careful around the ankles. Think of that space like the tender underside where your jaw turns to neck.

Please don't let anyone convince you that I will be cured of this disease if a swarm of bees stings me. I know not to swat. I've made an art of being careful.

As our pets age, please don't scold our old German Shepherd who loses control of her bowels. Show the old girl mercy, lift her nose from its angle toward the floor. Remember how she fishtails through the yard. Consider the tail she can no longer move, how it hangs like a dead branch when it used to wag.

When it thunders, I want to be wheeled to the porch. It is okay—even preferable—if the rain turns sideways and soaks my hair. I want to watch lightning over the church steeples. You don't have to stay outside with me when the sun goes down and the mosquitos start their long drain, but please light a candle and offer me a book.

Open the curtains each morning, please. Even, and especially, in winter. I want to see what I can't feel—shadows on snow dunes, shoe tracks on sidewalks—and know it is all still there. Ask me to shovel the walkway and pretend I've done it. Thank me, please, for the mulligatawny you've made for dinner, and remind me how it makes the house smell, like those old days. Give me time to blow on each spoonful before you tip it to my mouth.

SAFE ASHORE

You enter the exam room for my first appointment. I don't anticipate your slumped gait. For you, this is just called walking. This is called your beautiful life, and for me, it appears a tragedy that has befallen you just before you entered the door.

It is you who enters. It is not Cerebral Palsy that appears in the exam room after knocking gently. It is you, a man in an LL Bean sweater over a starched button down, perhaps a father, who shakes my hand and listens to my heart, who stables himself on my shoulder while he checks my lungs, an established and respected doctor of the neurology unit. A spouse who needs a new pair of Doc Marten's.

You speak into an audio recorder instead of typing away at a computer. I see your face instead of the glow of a screen as you explain about the growing colony of cotton-like lesions on the MRI of my brain. I am a patient, not a disembodied voice over your shoulder. You are not the stenographer for this neurology appointment, and I am not your chore. I see your crooked smile and speckles of dandruff on your glasses, your day-glow Fitbit and tawny complexion.

You recommend the strongest medication with side effects that include *a rare brain infection that usually leads to death or severe disability*. I have let the word *rare* fall from the sentence in my understanding of the drug, and say *No*.

A slick of saliva falls from your mouth to the linoleum floor, and I don't know why, but I apologize. When I realize how ridiculous it is to have apologized, I don't look you in the eyes. I want to wipe the thick suds from the floor with a paper towel from the mini sink. I want to dab your chin and ask you, my doctor, to rest on the exam table, if I can get you a cup of tea. Strawberry Jell-o? Some broth?

You don't adjust your gaze to the floor after I apologize. The saliva is of no matter to you, perhaps because I am in front of you, your patient, and you are a human doing your job, continuing to recommend a medication you believe will limit my own growing and, perhaps inevitable, disability. You will leave me the glossy literature on the medication, which features a sea of incredibly happy faces and testimonials. Attached to it, a new pen, branded swag.

You will give me time, call me later in the week to see if I've reconsidered the treatment. To you, it might seem as though you are throwing me a life raft—you know what lurks in the depths of this lake. I will be standing in my dining room, having just ruffled my son's hair, for now, safe ashore.

ACKNOWLEDGMENTS

Grateful acknowledgment is made to the editors of the following journals in which these works, or earlier versions of them, first appeared:

The Journal: "The Healer"

Under the Gum Tree: "On Small"

The Baltimore Review: "Aftermath"

Clockhouse: "A Picture of Natural Demise"

Punctuate: "On the Road's Shoulder"

The Citron Review: "re turn"

Brevity: "Future Instructions for Your Wife with Multiple Sclerosis"

Stonecoast Review: "Safe Ashore"

Sarah Cedeño's work has appeared in *Brevity*, *The Journal*, *2 Bridges*, *The Pinch*, *The Baltimore Review*, *The Rumpus*, *Hippocampus Magazine*, *Bellevue Literary Review*, and elsewhere. Sarah holds an MFA from Goddard College. She lives in Brockport, NY, with her husband and two sons, some old ghosts, and a dog, and she teaches writing at SUNY College at Brockport. You can visit her at www.sarahmcedeno.com.

Made in the USA
Coppell, TX
22 November 2022

86841457R10031